The Rockwool Foundation Research Unit

The significance of immigration for public finances in Denmark

Christer Gerdes,
Marie Louise Schultz-Nielsen
and Eskil Wadensjö

University Press of Southern Denmark
Odense 2011

The significance of immigration
for public finances in Denmark

Study Paper No. 35

Published by:
© The Rockwool Foundation Research Unit and
University Press of Southern Denmark

Copying from this book is permitted only within
institutions that have agreements with CopyDan,
and only in accordance with the limitations laid
down in the agreement

Address:
The Rockwool Foundation Research Unit
Sølvgade 10
DK-1307 Copenhagen K

Telephone   +45 33 34 48 00

Fax   +45 33 34 48 99

E-mail   forskningsenheden@rff.dk

Home page   www.rff.dk

ISBN 978-87-90199-59-3
ISSN 0908-3979
September 2011
Print run: 300
Printed by   Specialtrykkeriet Viborg A/S

Price: 60.00 DKK, including 25% VAT

Contents

Abstract: 5
1. International migration affects a number of parties. 6
2. Different types of immigration 7
3. The economic effects experienced by immigration
   host countries 10
4. The effects on public finances 11
5. Data 14
6. The components of net transfers in 2004. 16
7. Redistribution of income between various age groups in 2004 19
8. Total net transfers 1991-2004 21
9. Estimated net transfers for the period 2005-2008 24
10. Summary 28
Appendix 1. Definition of refugees 30
References 31

The significance of immigration for public finances in Denmark

Christer Gerdes[1], Marie Louise Schultz-Nielsen[2] and Eskil Wadensjö[1]

Abstract:

This paper studies the economic consequences of immigration for public finances in Denmark. Using new figures for the period 2004-2008, net transfers are calculated, and presented as an extension to the figures that already existed for the period 1991-2001. The net transfers are calculated from a marginal perspective, which means that the included public expenditures and incomes can be traced to each individual person in our sample. The study is therefore suited for analyzing the economic consequences if more/less people immigrate. A consistent pattern to emerge throughout is that net transfers from Western first- and second-generation immigrants to state funds are positive, while those from non-Western first- and second-generation immigrants are negative. The new calculations show that net transfers from non-Western first- and second-generation immigrants fell in absolute terms from DKK -12.8 billion in 2004 to DKK -9.1 billion in 2008, largely due to the improved employment situation in Denmark. The results also show that the composition chosen of the group of non-Western immigrants has a significant effect on the calculation of net transfers, in that these transfers are reduced to DKK -2.2 billion if refugees are excluded from this group.

---

1 Swedish Institute for Social Research (SOFI), Stockholm University.
2 Rockwool Foundation Research Unit, Copenhagen.

1. International migration affects a number of parties

Migration across international borders affects a number of parties: the people who emigrate, the country to which they emigrate, and the country they leave. The consequences are, of course, greatest for the people who make the migration, but the effects can also be of considerable significance for the countries involved.

For the migrants themselves, the decision to emigrate usually has major consequences, but it can have great significance for members of their families as well. The migrants have decided that leaving is a better solution than staying where they are. 'Better' might refer to purely financial considerations, but it could also mean an improvement in political or social situation. Many people migrate not to obtain better paid work, but to escape from political oppression or to be reunited with members of their families. Even though the migrants expect that they will achieve an improvement in their situations, the results can in fact prove to be otherwise. Incorrect or incomplete information about conditions in the country to which they are migrating may be one reason for this, while changes in conditions in the countries of origin and destination can constitute another explanation. The short- and long-term effects of migration can also vary greatly. Research into international migration often focuses on the outcomes for the migrants. What is the nature of the integration process? What differences are there among various individuals and groups of people, and among different countries? But outcomes are of significance not only for the migrants themselves; they also affect the receiving country. Better integration can affect the public finances of the country, for example.

There are also effects on the countries that migrants leave, including both economic and political effects. Wages, income from capital, profits, employment, and public sector finances can all be affected: often in the opposite direction to the effects in the receiving country. In migration source countries, there is often concern about a 'brain drain' – the departure from the country of large numbers of highly-educated people whose education has been paid for by the country they leave. Birth rates are low in the new EU member states in Central and Eastern Europe, and the percentages of people in the populations who are of working age are growing smaller. Emigration can exacerbate the consequences of these trends, and make the problems of balancing the budget even greater. This is, naturally, a cause for concern. On the other hand, transfers of money to the home country from emigrants and increased skills among returning migrants can bolster the country's economic development and help to counteract the negative effects of emigration.

Our focus in this study, however, is on the consequences for Denmark as a receiving country for immigration. We will limit ourselves to an examination of the economic consequences, and in particular those that are of significance for public finances.

Research into the economic consequences of immigration typically distinguishes between three types of effects: effects on wages for the existing population, employment effects for the existing population, and effects on public finances.[3] There are also other economic effects of immigration, of course, such as the effects on company profits, investments, capital returns, prices and innovation. However, few research results are available for effects of these types.

It is important to note that there are relationships between the various effects, since all parts of a nation's economy are interconnected. If there are changes to wages, profits and employment, there will be an indirect effect on public finances, since the tax base will change. If one focuses exclusively on a particular type of effect without taking the indirect consequences into account, then one sees only a part of the larger picture. It can, of course, be both productive and interesting to focus on one effect, but it is important to be aware of the limitations of this: it is not possible to achieve an account of the overall effects in this way.

2. Different types of immigration

In any analysis of the economic effects of immigration, it is important to bear in mind that there are various types of immigrants, whose goals in migrating are different, and whose opportunities for success in the host country are also different. In consequence, it is also to be expected that the effects of immigration will differ according to the type of immigration. In the following, we will briefly consider the most important forms of immigration and some of the effects that can be expected.

1. *Labour immigration* (or economic immigration) This type of immigration, for a long time the dominant immigration type in Europe, comprised the immigration of labour. In Sweden, this type of immigration was already of significance in the second half of the 1940s, whereas other countries in Western Europe, including Denmark, first received large numbers of labour immigrants in the 1960s. Many people migrated to Western European countries from the Mediterranean region (Southern Europe and Turkey) and from Finland and Ireland. At the same time, there was significant immigration from former colonies in Africa, Asia and the West Indies to the respective colonial powers (principally Belgium, France, the Netherlands and the United Kingdom), though also to other countries. The immigrants came to seek employment, and

---

[3] For two recent overviews of research into the economic consequences of immigration, see Bodvarsson and Van den Berg (2009) and Pekkala Kerr and Kerr (2011).

were thus of working age. This type of migration was often described in the 1960s as the arrival of guest workers. The expectation was that the 'guests' would stay for some years, and then return home. There were indeed many who did precisely that – the later remigration was of no small significance in scale – but many others stayed on in the host countries, and these were frequently joined later by members of their families. The simple logic behind the guest worker system was that the migrants would be able to begin work straight away in the host country, and that they would leave the country again long before they reached retirement age. They contributed to the public sector by paying tax, but they did not have much impact on public spending, which meant that they were net contributors to public finances. Another positive result for the host countries, which was much discussed at the time, was that access to an 'unlimited' supply of labour meant that companies invested more than they would otherwise have done. The positive effects thus continued, in that companies' profits were then greater, which naturally meant that they paid more in tax.

Concurrently with the large-scale migration of labour, primarily from south to north, came the construction of common labour markets. The first of these was the Common Nordic Labour Market, which was officially established in 1954. Next came the European Economic Community's common labour market (later the EU common labour market), which was set up in three stages in the 1960s, and which has since been expanded several times through the accession of new member states. Today, a common labour market exists for citizens of the 27 EU member states (with certain transitional regulations in force in some immigration-receiving countries which apply to nationals of the most recent member states), the member states in the Common Nordic Labour Market, the member states of the European Economic Area, and one state with an agreement with the EEA (Switzerland). The arguments in favour of common labour markets have been primarily economic – free movement of labour, like free movement of goods and services, capital and businesses, should result in increased economic prosperity for the countries with access to such common markets.

Labour immigrants are normally capable of participating in the labour market, and a relatively high percentage of them are in employment. Labour immigrants move to countries where there are jobs available. This type of migration is highly dependent on the business cycle – it is much more prevalent during periods of economic prosperity.

2. *Refugee immigration.* Refugees constitute the second large group of immigrants. Refugees migrate for political rather than economic reasons, the political situation in their home countries being the deciding factor in their migration. This means that many arrive in their host countries without the skills and the

experience required by the labour market there, or they arrive during a period of high unemployment. The motivation for a country to accept refugees is humanitarian rather than economic. It can be compared with overseas aid – countries do not give such aid to reap economic benefits, but to help the vulnerable. Nevertheless, there often exist politically-motivated goals for reducing the costs to the public purse of accepting refugees. The successful integration of refugees that places them in a better position to succeed on the labour market not only leads to a better situation for the refugees themselves, but also helps to lower the costs to the public sector. This saving might mean, for example, that the country concerned can accept a greater number of refugees without increasing the financial costs of doing so.

The fact that refugees come to a country for reasons of political necessity does not mean that they cannot work and contribute to society, depending to a large extent on their skills and state of health. The refugees who came to the USA from Germany during the 1930s constitute one example of the rapid integration of refugees into the labour market; they helped to make the United States the leading nation in the world for scientific research. Another such example is provided by the refugees who came from Denmark, Estonia and Norway to Sweden during the Second World War; they were able to start work immediately. This was also the case for the refugees who migrated from Hungary to Sweden in 1956 and from Poland and Czechoslovakia to Sweden in 1968. They did not always find work that matched their education, however. This was the situation for lawyers, for example, who could not obtain the necessary permits to work within their field. In other ways, too, refugee immigrants differ from labour immigrants; for example, refugees are generally rather older.

3. *Family reunification.* The third large immigrant group consists of members of the families of earlier immigrants. When a country accepts these family immigrants, it is normally neither for labour market reasons nor on political grounds. The reasoning in this case is linked to human rights and the respect for family live – the principle that families should be able to live together. This means that most countries accept the principle that close family members of refugees and labour immigrants (spouses and children who are minors) should be reunited with the people who initially moved to the country (usually the male head of the family). The definition applied of 'close family members' varies from country to country, and over time. One sub-group of family reunification immigrants consists of people who have at times been referred to as 'marriage immigrants'. These immigrants apply for permission to immigrate when entering into a marriage. In this area, the rules vary even more from country to country, and over time. Family reunification immigrants and marriage immigrants may find it easy or difficult to find work in the host country. This is dependent on their education and work experience to a large

extent, but it is also of great importance whether or not their family members already in the country can support them in their job search.

4. *Students.* Most economically highly developed countries receive many students from other countries in connection with programmes of higher education. This migration of students is most significant in English-speaking countries. The various countries have widely differing policies regarding the opportunities that students are given to stay on in the country after their education is finished. These policies, too, have changed over time. In some countries, students are required to return to their home countries immediately after completion of their education, while other countries make it easy for those who can find work to stay on. In countries of the latter type, the process is often regarded as a 'brain gain' – a special form of labour immigration.

In analyses in this research field, immigrants are frequently divided into Western and non-Western immigrants. Such a division can provide very useful information, but can also be wildly misleading in certain contexts. Immigrants from non-Western countries may be labour immigrants, refugees, family reunification immigrants or students, and thus be migrating in very different circumstances. We shall return to this point in the analysis of net financial transfers, but for the time being we shall simply illustrate the nature of the issue with an example from Sweden. Here, a change in the law that came into force on 15 December 2008 has led to an increase in the immigration of IT specialists and engineers from India and China. These people come to the country in order to work, and it is not expected that they will have any difficulty in continuing to find employment on the Swedish labour market.

3. The economic effects experienced by immigration host countries

The effects of immigration are widely discussed in Western countries, from both political and academic perspectives. The debate concerns not only economic effects but also cultural, political and social consequences of immigration. Positions taken are often based more on opinions than facts, so it is important that further research should be conducted in these areas. It is also very important that there should be research into the economic consequences of immigration. In this area, too, there are exaggerated ideas about the significance of immigration. At the same time, this is not an easy field for research. International migration can affect all aspects of an economy. Moreover, economies are subject to constant changes that have nothing to do with immigration, as Rothman and Espenshade (1992) point out. Thus, it can be difficult to isolate the significance of immigration. This is especially true in relation to the effects of immigration on wages; there has been extensive debate among researchers as to the best methods of investigating these effects. However, most studies indicate that the effects are small. The same applies to the consequences for employment of the rest of the population. This can be explained in part by the fact that, the immigrant population and the rest of the population do different types of work, and thus are complements in the production process rather than substitutes. Another aspect of the explanation lies in the fact that immigration results in greater investment. There are also a number of studies of the effects of immigration on public finances. This type of research also has its fair share of methodological complications.[4] We will consider these issues more fully below.

4. The effects on public finances

The finances of the public sector – both income and expenditure – are affected in various ways by changes to the population due to immigration. The sum of these changes represents the marginal gain/loss of a change in migration inflow. In order to understand the underlying mechanisms of these processes, it is relevant to divide public finances up into taxes, transfers and public consumption.

If the population increases because of immigration, tax revenue will also increase. People in employment pay income tax, and those who have incomes from capital are also taxed. In addition, there are various taxes related to consumption such as VAT and special taxes and duties, and tax is also payable on certain transfer incomes. Most tax income is directly linked to individuals, and can thus also be linked to specific population groups, such as immigrants. The exception to this is company taxation, which is often difficult to link to individuals.

In many ways it is even easier to link transfer incomes to individuals than it is to make the links for taxes, since the majority of transfer incomes are paid to individuals. This applies, for example, in the cases of unemployment benefit, sickness benefit, disability pensions and old age pensions. The exception – again – is transfers to companies, for example in the form of various forms of subsidy.

---

4 The references section lists many of the studies that have been undertaken concerning net transfers to or from the public finances. For previous studies of Denmark, see Wadensjö (2000, 2000a), Wadensjö and Orrje (2002), Wadensjö and Gerdes (2004), Gerdes and Wadensjö (2006), Wadensjö (2007) and in relation to the EU enlargement, see Malchow-Møller et al. (2009). Studies related to other countries include: for Australia, Ablett (1991); for Canada, Akbari (1991); for Italy, Moscarola (2001); for Norway, ECON (1996) and Larsen and Bruce (1998); for Spain, Collado et al. (2004); for Sweden, Wadensjö (1973), Ekberg (1983, 1999, 2009), Storesletten (1998, 2003) and Gustafsson and Österberg (2001); for Germany, Bonin et al. (2000), Bonin (2002) and Wadensjö and Gerdes (2004); and for the USA, Simon (1984), Rothman and Espenshade (1992), Clune (1992), Garvey and Espenshade (1998), Lee and Miller (1998), McCurdy et al. (1998), Auerbach and Oreopoulos (1999) and Storesletten (2002).

The most difficult thing is to link public sector consumption and public investment to individuals. Some expenditure is easy to link to individuals, provided the appropriate data is accessible; this is true, for example, with regard to social expenditures as health care and care for the elderly, and to the cost of places on courses of education. Other expenditures can be divided equally between all members of the population, or between all the people living in a given municipality; the latter is true, for example, in the case of municipal investments in the road network, which can be assumed to increase with the number of inhabitants. Other budget items can be harder to allocate among individuals, either because it is difficult to identify an appropriate principle for the distribution of the costs, or because the expenditure is for a 'public good' where the costs do not increase with the size of the population.

Where expenditures are independent of the size of the population, however, it may be incorrect to include them in the analysis at all. If the question to be answered is 'What are the economic consequences of an increased or diminished flow of immigrants?', then the marginal change in costs to the public sector of increased or decreased immigration will be zero in relation to the cost of a public good. On the other hand, one might reason that without any population at all there would be no such costs, which is an argument for averaging them among all individual members of the population.

In the present study, only the expenditures and incomes for the public sector that can be clearly linked to individuals, as outlined above, are taken into account; and these are allocated to the individuals concerned. It would probably be beneficial to the study if a larger proportion of public costs could be allocated on an individual level. Immigration is hardly a marginal phenomenon any longer, and public expenditures such as those on roads, administration and defence do vary to a certain extent with the size of the population. The ideal solution would therefore be to make calculations on both marginal and average bases. However, this has not been possible with the existing data.

In general, more of public income than public expenditure can be linked to individuals, and thus to population groups. As a result, this type of calculation tends to suggest a surplus, even if the public sector finances should be in balance. Consequently, it is not unusual to focus on how net transfers to public finances differ among those for various groups in the population, and in this way to analyse each group's relative contribution.

What, then, can we expect to find when we consider the structure of net transfers? Redistribution of income in a welfare society flows mainly from people of working age to children and young people, and to the elderly. In the case of children and young people, this is mainly a question of expenditures on day nurseries, preschools, schools and further education (i.e. public consumption) and, to a lesser extent, on transfer incomes (generally made to the parents). In the case of the elderly, expenditures are both on transfer incomes (pensions) and public consumption (health care and old age care). The other type of redistribution in a welfare society flows between people of working age, from those who are in employment to those who – for reasons of illness, unemployment or on other grounds – are not.

Taken over the whole population divided into groups by age, the pattern found is of negative transfers in the case of children, young people and the elderly and positive transfers for the age groups in between, where people are active on the labour market. We can also expect to find differences that depend on whether people were born in the country in question or in another country. This will be true especially among people of working age, whose rate of employment in the case of immigrants can be expected to depend on the qualifications they have and their reasons for immigrating to the country, i.e. whether they were labour immigrants or refugees.

This pattern does not tell us how large the total net transfers are, however. The amounts are dependent to a high degree on the age compositions of the various groups. A group made up of a large proportion of people of working age will produce a larger positive net transfer than a group with fewer people of working age, even if the net transfer per person of a given age is the same. Figure 1 shows that immigrants from Western countries include relatively few children and young people, but a relatively large percentage of people of working age.[5] Immigrant groups from non-Western countries are made up of a large proportion of relatively young working-age people, and also of many children and young people – but very few elderly people. The majority of non-Western immigrants arrived in Denmark within the past two decades, which is, on average, significantly later than is the case for the Western immigrant group.

When calculations are made of net transfers for the various groups, it is common practice to do this as an average for the groups over the course of a particular year or a specific period of several years. There is, however, a problem with this approach. If one considers a group of people who came to the country a long time ago – i.e. when they were young – and who have now reached retirement age, one will undoubtedly find a large net transfer to this group, despite the fact that they may have contributed positively in the years before the period covered by the study. One possible solution is to include children and, if possible, grandchildren in the calculation, so that the analysis is not focused on the net transfers associated with an individual immigrant alone, but instead takes into account the whole of the

---

5 A more detailed description of the data basis for the division into Western and non-Western immigrants is provided in Section 5.

contribution made as a result of that person's immigration. Another solution is to perform a cohort calculation, which involves considering the total net transfers made by a cohort – in this case, the immigrants who came to the country in a given year.[6] This type of calculation requires access to very good and accurate data that cover a period of many years and to reliable prognoses for the future trends for the group, unless the study concentrates exclusively on immigration cohorts that arrived in the country many years previously.

Figure 1. The age composition of population groups, according to areas of origin. 2004.

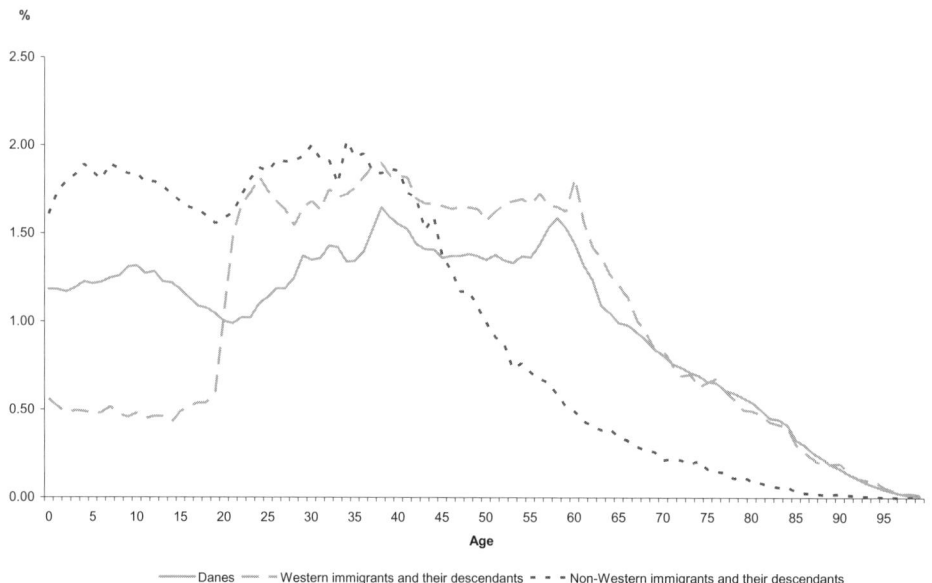

——— Danes — — Western immigrants and their descendants - - - Non-Western immigrants and their descendants

Note: The calculations are based on moving averages of three years.
Source: Own calculations based on the Danish Finance Ministry's Law Model.

5. Data

We have used data from the Danish Ministry of Finance's Law Model to calculate net transfers and the various components of these for the year 2004. A detailed description of the methodology can be found in Wadensjö and Orrje (2002) and Wadensjö and Gerdes (2004). We do not have Law Model data for more recent years, but on the basis of the relation between net transfers and a series of factors, including level of activity on the labour market, we have estimated the values of net transfers for the years 2005-2008. It is interesting to trace this development,

---

6 Two examples of studies that make use of such cohort calculations are Ablett (1999) and Auerbach and Oreopoulus (1999).

since the size of net transfers for an individual are closely linked to that person's employment situation, and employment rates – including those for non-Western immigrants – changed markedly (for the better) during that period. The information used to make this extrapolation came from the registers at Statistics Denmark.

The analysis is based on a division of the Danish population on the basis of places of origin. We make a distinction between people originating from Denmark, from Western countries and from non-Western countries. The Western countries are comprised of Andorra, Iceland, Liechtenstein, Monaco, Norway, San Marino, Switzerland, the Vatican state, Canada, the USA, Australia and New Zealand, in addition to the 15 countries that were EU member states prior to 2004 (though excluding Denmark). The new EU member states are not counted among the Western countries in order to allow comparison of the results for 2004 and onwards with those from earlier periods. It is possible to distinguish between people originating in countries other than Denmark according to whether they are original immigrants or second generation immigrants. This has been done here using Statistics Denmark's definitions.[7]

Table 1 provides an overview of the Danish population divided according to origin, as the situation was at the end of 2004. It shows that, of the 5.4 million people resident in Denmark at that time, 91.6 percent were Danes, i.e. people who were neither original immigrants nor second-generation immigrants. People of Western origin (including second-generation immigrants) made up 2 percent of the population, while people of non-Western origin constituted 6.3 percent.

Table 1. The population of Denmark at the end of 2004, divided according to origin.

	Number	Percentage
Danes	4,959,310	91.6
Western immigrants and second-generation immigrants	110,762	2.0
Non-Western immigrants and second-generation immigrants	341,333	6.3
– of whom, refugees	170,322	3.1
– of whom, non-refugees	171,011	3.2
Total	5,411,405	100.0

Source: Own calculations based on registers at Statistics Denmark.

---

7 Immigrants are defined as people born outside Denmark of parents who were both either non-Danish nationals or born outside Denmark. Second-generation immigrants are defined as people born in Denmark of parents neither of whom was a Danish citizen born in Denmark. See Danmarks Statistik (2010).

An attempt has been made to sub-divide the group comprising people of non-Western origin into refugees and non-refugees. This sub-division results in around half the non-Western immigrants being categorised as refugees, and half as non-refugees. The division has been made on the basis of information about the country of origin and the time of immigration, since information about the grounds for granting a residence permit is not available for all immigrants. Since refugees are often married to fellow-nationals, and since we do not differentiate between which of the couple arrived first, the group also includes family members arriving for reunification with refugees. This is appropriate in this analysis, since the immigration of these family members is initiated by the arrival of the refugees. Also second-generation immigrants are included among the refugees. Further details relating to the definition of refugees are given in Appendix 1.

6. The components of net transfers in 2004

We present our report in stages, beginning with the results of the calculations for each of the components that together constitute net transfers, namely taxes, transfer incomes and public consumption.

The first of these three components is taxes. The relationship between age and tax payments in Denmark is shown in Figure 2. As is to be expected, children pay no tax, having no income. Generally speaking, people begin to receive a taxable income as teenagers. As the figure shows, tax payments per person rise up until around 45 years of age, after which point they gradually decline. The curve levels out at around age 65. Pensioners do pay tax, but their incomes are lower, and their tax payments are therefore also lower than for people of working age.

The curve for Western immigrants follows the curve for Danes relatively closely. The largest deviation is for young people. The reason for this is that a relatively large proportion of Western immigrants in these age groups are students. The curve for non-Western immigrants is clearly below those for the two other groups, which is due to a combination of a lower rate of participation in the labour market, a higher level of unemployment, and lower rates of pay. The large fluctuations in the levels for elderly non-Western immigrants are due to the fact that there are only a small number of people in these age groups, with the result that single observations have a large effect on the averages.

Figure 2. Tax payments per person by age and place of origin, 2004.

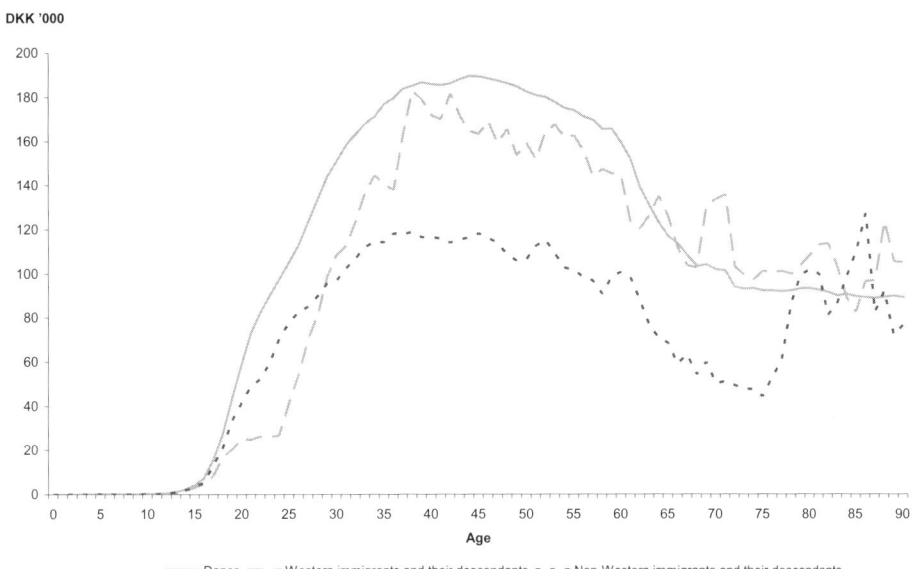

Note: The calculations are based on moving averages of three years.
Source: Own calculations based on the Danish Finance Ministry's Law Model.

The next component is transfer incomes, which are shown in Figure 3. There are no transfers to children, since payments that are related to the children in a family are made to the parents. Here again, there are no major discrepancies between Danes and Western immigrants in the age range 35-60. The clearest differences are among younger people and the elderly. For both these groups, transfers to Danes are larger than those to immigrants from Western countries. In the case of the elderly, the difference is primarily due to the payment of early retirement benefit (up until age 65) and old age pensions; and for the younger group, the difference is related to payments related to study (Danish students are entitled to economic support from the Danish State, which is not always the case for immigrants) and level of activity on the labour market.

For people in the age range 25-63, transfers to non-Western immigrants are significantly greater than those to Danes. The proportion of people in employment is smaller for this group, and the average number of children is greater, which means that the members of this group receive more unemployment benefit or social assistance and more child support payments than Danes.

6. The components of net transfers in 2004

Figure 3. Transfer incomes per person by age and place of origin, 2004.

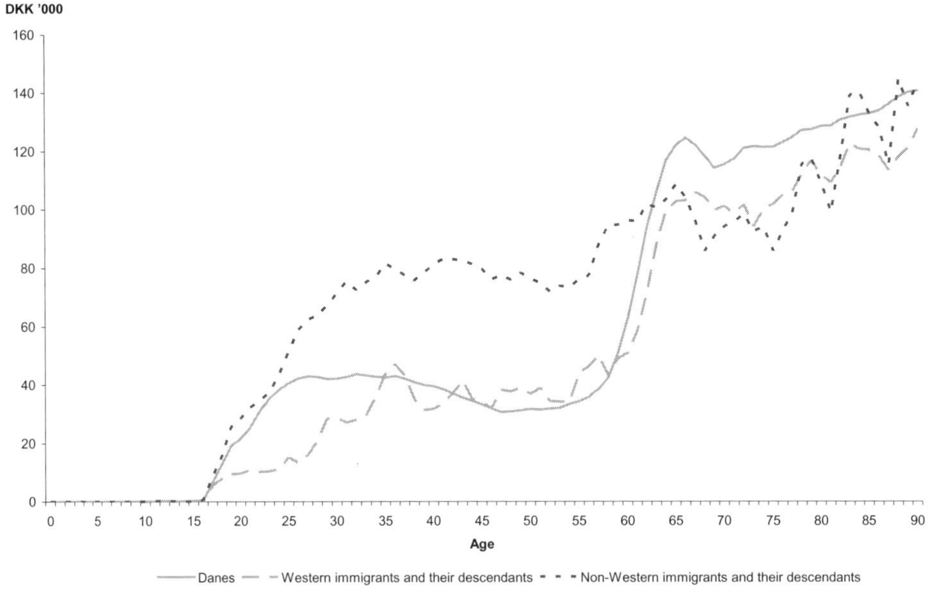

Note: The calculations are based on moving averages of three years.
Source: Own calculations based on the Danish Finance Ministry's Law Model.

The third component in the calculation of net transfers is public consumption; see Figure 4. Expenditures are highest for the young (costs of child care and education) and the elderly (costs of health care and care of the elderly). Here, the expenditure levels for the three groups are relatively close, although expenditures are somewhat higher for non-Western immigrants than for Danes between the ages of 25 and 65. The large variations in public consumption in the graph line for non-Western immigrants at the older age levels are due to the fact that there are few such older immigrants from non-Western countries, and thus individual observations make large differences to the averages.

Figure 4. Public consumption per person by age and place of origin, 2004.

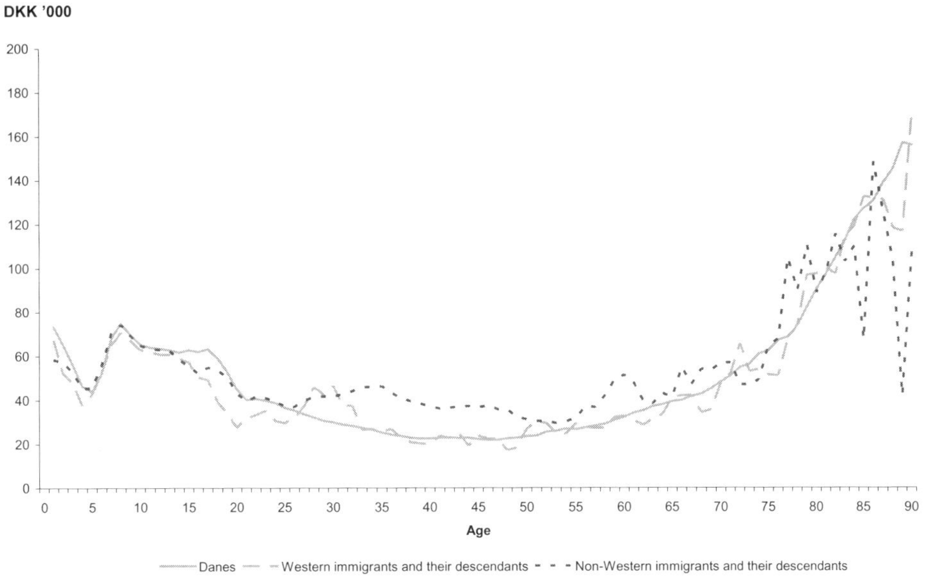

Note: The calculations are based on moving averages of three years.
Source: Own calculations based on the Danish Finance Ministry's Law Model.

7. Redistribution of income between various age groups in 2004

What, then, is the situation regarding net transfers for the various age groups? In order to answer this question, we have calculated the differences between taxes paid and the sum of transfer incomes and public consumption; see Figure 5. The curves for Danes and Western immigrants follow each other closely. In the case of non-Western immigrants, the curve is also close to that for Danes for people under the age of 20 and for those over the age of 70. However, net transfers are not positive on average for non-Western immigrants of working age. Instead, they are at around the zero point. This is largely due to the fact that rates of employment are lower for non-Western immigrants.

Figure 5. Net transfers per person to the public finances in Denmark, by age and place of origin, 2004.

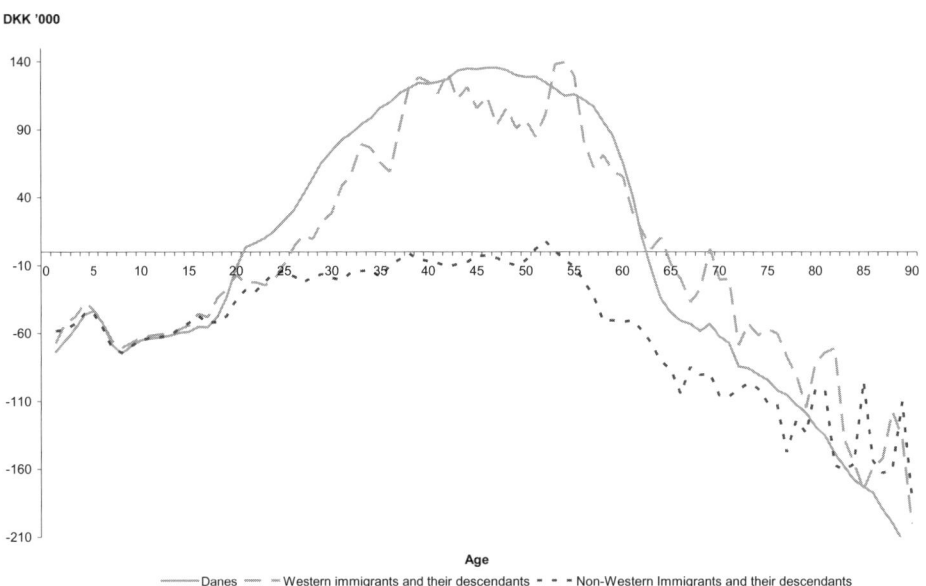

Note: The calculations are based on moving averages of three years.
Source: Own calculations based on the Danish Finance Ministry's Law Model.

There is a lively public debate in Denmark regarding how the children of immigrants, and particularly the children of non-Western immigrants, fare in life in comparison with children whose parents were born in Denmark. The vast majority of second-generation non-Western immigrants are still young, and therefore it is not yet possible to study their situation in the later stages of life. On the other hand, it is possible to compare the levels of net transfers for younger people in relation to the origins of their parents. Figure 6 shows that net transfers up until the age of 30 are approximately the same for those people whose parents were born in Denmark as for those whose parents were born in non-Western countries. This is also true to some extent for people whose parents were born in other Western countries. This pattern may be the result of a process of integration, with the young second-generation immigrants coming to lead lives that are more similar to those of the rest of the population. Integration research also reveals clear signs that the patterns of educational choices, employment and family formation of second-generation immigrants are moving closer to those of the rest of the population, though there are still differences in certain respects, see Tranæs (2008) and Schultz-Nielsen (2010).

Figure 6. Net transfers per person to the public finances among young people born in Denmark, 2004.

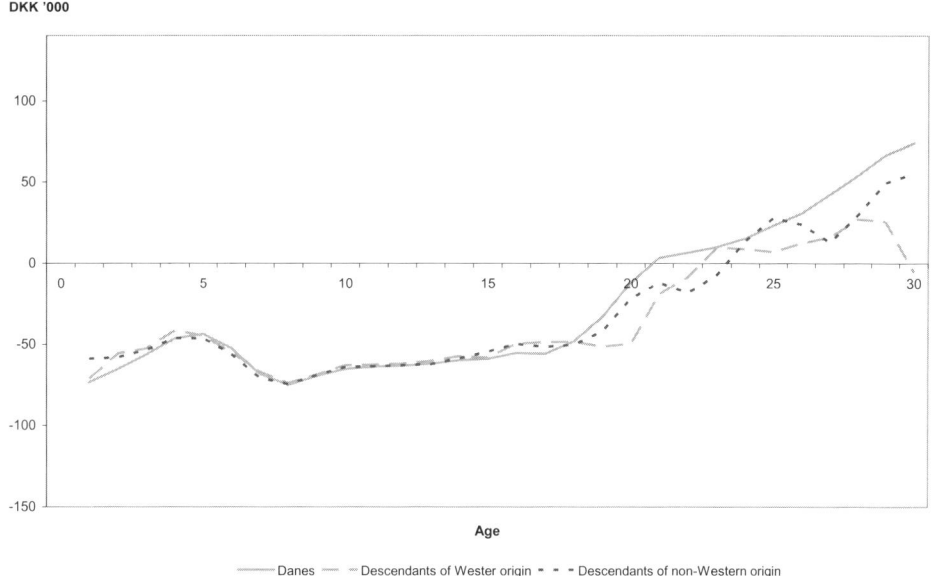

Note: The calculations are based on moving averages of three years.
Source: Own calculations based on the Danish Finance Ministry's Law Model.

8. Total net transfers 1991-2004

The figures presented in the previous section illustrated the relationships between net transfers and age, related to place of origin; but these figures provided no direct information about the average size of the net transfers for any given group. This average depends to a large part on the age composition of the group in question. What is the composition of each group in terms of age? Figure 1 showed considerable differences among the three groups in relation to age composition. In order to calculate total net transfers to or from public finances, it is also necessary to take into account the size of each group. First, however, we shall examine average figures for the period 1991-2004; these are presented in Table 2. The figures for the period 1991-2001 have previously been presented in Gerdes and Wadensjö (2006), but those for 2004 are new.

The table shows that there were no great changes between 2001 and 2004. For Danes, there was a decrease in the average net transfers to the public purse from DKK 30,400 per person in 2001 to DKK 30,200 in 2004; this corresponds to a slightly greater fall measured in fixed prices. For Western immigrants there was a considerable decrease in net transfers; for immigrants and their children taken together, the decrease was from DKK 42,300 in 2001 to DKK 25,600 in 2004,[8] whereas the corresponding figures for the non-Western group were DKK -54,200 and DKK -55,200. As the table shows, there was a tendency throughout the period for net transfers to be positive for Western immigrants, but negative for non-Western immigrants. For Western immigrants, the amounts were approximately the same as for Danes. The amounts are clearly the largest for the children of Western immigrants, while those for the children of non-Western immigrants are negative. The large differences between these groups can be ascribed first and foremost to the considerable differences in the age compositions of the groups. Second-generation non-Western immigrants, as mentioned previously, are generally young and just starting out on the labour market.

Table 2. Net transfers to the public finances (in DKK) per person over the age of 18, by place of origin, 1991-2004. Amounts in 1997 prices are stated in italics.

	1991	1995	1996	1997	1998	1999	2000	2001	2004
				DKK					
Danes	13,400	14,800	18,600	22,300	24,500	26,700	29,000	30,400	30,200
	14,800	*15,600*	*18,600*		*23,800*	*25,200*	*27,500*	*28,200*	*26,000*
Western immigrants	14,800	14,100	11,100	12,600	23,800	25,200	39,300	40,800	22,400
	15,600	*14,800*	*11,100*		*23,000*	*23,800*	*37,100*	*37,100*	*19,300*
Western second-generation immigrants	19,300	8,900	26,700	34,200	19,300	40,100	50,500	55,700	65,300
	21,500	*9,700*	*27,500*		*19,300*	*37,900*	*46,800*	*50,500*	*56,400*
All Western immigrants	14,800	14,100	11,900	14,800	23,800	26,000	40,800	42,300	25,600
	16,300	*14,800*	*12,600*		*23,000*	*25,200*	*37,900*	*38,600*	*22,100*
Non-Western immigrants	-49,000	-65,300	-66,100	-60,900	-54,200	-55,700	-58,600	-57,900	-58,900
	-53,500	*-53,300*	*-67,600*		*-53,500*	*-53,500*	*-54,900*	*-52,700*	*-50,800*
Non-Western second-generation immigrants	700	-19,300	-16,300	-18,600	-700	-19,300	-14,100	-4,500	-7,100
	700	*-20,000*	*-16,300*		*-700*	*-18,600*	*-13,400*	*-3,700*	*-6,100*
All non-Western immigrants	-48,300	-63,800	-63,800	-58,600	-52,000	-54,200	-55,700	-54,200	-55,200
	-52,700	*-66,100*	*-65,300*		*-50,500*	*-52,000*	*-52,000*	*-49,700*	*-47,600*
Total	11,900	12,600	14,800	19,300	21,500	23,000	25,200	26,700	27,700
	13,400	*12,600*	*15,600*		*20,800*	*22,300*	*23,800*	*24,500*	*23,900*

Note: Western countries are defined as the EU member states (EU15, excluding Denmark), Norway, Switzerland, Iceland, North American countries, Australia and New Zealand; non-Western countries are all other countries.

Source: Own calculations based on the Danish Finance Ministry's Law Model.

---

[8] The decrease related only to Western immigrants, and not to their children, for whom net transfers actually increased. Part of the reason for the fall may have been that the proportion of Western immigrants reaching retirement age increased.

The next stage is to calculate total net transfers to the public finances on the basis of average net transfers per person and the size of each group. The results of this calculation are presented in Table 3.

Table 3. Net transfers to the public finances (in DKK), by place of origin, 1991-2004. Amounts in 1997 prices are stated in italics.

	1991	1995	1996	1997	1998	1999	2000	2001	2004
	-- DKK, millions --								
Western[1] immigrants	1,046 *1,151*	1,143 *1,188*	913 *928*	1,054	2,101 *2,064*	2,205 *2,163*	3,460 *3,229*	3,601 *3,289*	2,086 *1,797*
Western second-generation immigrants	126 *134*	67 *67*	208 *208*	252	141 *134*	304 *290*	401 *379*	453 *408*	505 *438*
All Western immigrants	1,173 *1,284*	1,203 *1,255*	1,121 *1,143*	1,307	2,242 *2,198*	2,509 *2,405*	3,868 *3,608*	4,040 *3,705*	2,598 *2,242*
Non-Western immigrants	-4,855 *-5,338*	-8,753 *-9,206*	-9,488 *-9,763*	-9,132	-8,790 *-8,597*	-9,436 *-9,191*	-10,631 *-10,060*	-11,077 *-10,149*	-12,732 *-10,988*
Non-Western second-generation immigrants	1 *1*	-82 *-82*	-74 *-74*	-104	15 *15*	-148 *-141*	-141 *-134*	-37 *-30*	-119 *-104*
All non-Western immigrants	-4,788 *-5,338*	-8,835 *-9,206*	-9,562 *-9,763*	-9,235	-8,775 *-8,597*	-9,577 *-9,191*	-10,772 *-10,060*	-11,114 *-10,149*	-12,844 *-11,084*
All immigrants[2]	-3,682 *-4,046*	-7,624 *-7,951*	-8,449 *-8,827*	-7,929	-6,533 *-6,399*	-7,068 *-6,785*	-6,904 *-6,451*	-7,060 *-6,444*	-10,245 *-8,308*
	-- As a percentage of GDP --								
All Western immigrants[2]	0.13	0.11	0.10	0.12	0.19	0.21	0.30	0.30	0.18
All non-Western immigrants[2]	-0.54	-0.88	-0.89	-0.83	-0.75	-0.79	-0.84	-0.83	-0.88
All immigrants[2]	-0.41	-0.76	-0.79	-0.71	-0.56	-0.58	-0.54	-0.53	-0.70

Notes: 1) Western countries are defined as the EU member states (EU15, excluding Denmark), Norway, Switzerland, Iceland, North American countries, Australia and New Zealand; non-Western countries are all other countries. 2) Including second-generation immigrants.

Source: Own calculations based on the Danish Finance Ministry's Law Model.

Total net transfers from Western immigrants and second-generation immigrants to public finances were positive at around DKK 2.6 billion in 2004, while the corresponding sum for non-Western immigrants and second-generation immigrants was negative at around DKK -12.8 billion. The total amounts for all immigrants and second-generation immigrants vary over the years in relation to GDP between 0.41 percent and 0.79 percent of GDP. In 2004, the total amount was equivalent to 0.70 percent of GDP.

Our results differ markedly from those recently calculated by DREAM and published by the Danish think-tank CEPOS (Lundby Hansen, 2011) and the Danish Government (2011). The greatest difference is in the figures for Danes, for whom DREAM reports much lower levels of net transfers to the public finances. The differences between DREAM's figures and ours are much smaller with respect to both Western and non-Western immigrants. The size of the difference is mainly due to DREAM having distributed a significantly greater proportion of the expenditures for public consumption, and these amounts have been allocated to Danes in particular based on the differences in the age composition between Danes and immigrant groups.

9. Estimated net transfers for the period 2005-2008

How has the situation changed since 2004? Using data on the compositions of the various groups, and taking into account socio-demographic characteristics and levels of activity on the labour market, we have extrapolated figures for the years 2005-2008.

Such calculations require that information is available for each individual on the factors used in the regressions. This information is available for the period up until the end of 2008, with the exception of information about net transfers, which is only available up until 2004. The first calculation, described in equation (1), is based on information for the year 2004. This allows an estimate of the correlation between the explanatory variables and net transfers. The model is shown in a version where individuals' places of origin are included in the regression on the same basis as other explanatory variables. To give the model greater flexibility, we also decided to make separate estimations for each of the three groups (Danes, Western immigrants and second-generation immigrants, and non-Western immigrants and second-generation immigrants). The results presented later are based on the latter specification of the model, but the results are fairly robust with respect to this change.

(1) $\text{Net transfers}_i = a_i + b_1 * \text{age}_i + b_2 * \text{age squared}_i + b_3 * \text{gender}_i + b_4 * \text{familystatus}_i + b_5 * \text{immigrantstatus}_i + b_6 * \text{education}_i + b_7 * \text{employmentstatus}_i$

The next stage is – on basis of the parameter estimates from the estimated model for 2004 – to predict the net transfers (in 2004 prices) for the years 2005-2008, where the values for the explanatory variables are inserted for the subsequent years.

In the third stage, we take the predicted values for the years 2005-2008 for each individual, add them together in their respective groups (i.e. Danes, Western and non-Western immigrants), and adjust the amounts to current prices.

Table 4 shows the average net transfers per person in current prices for the three groups. The most notable change is in the average net transfers to the public finances from non-Western immigrants, which go from DKK -55,200 in 2004 to DKK -53,300 in 2005 before finally declining to DKK -31,200 in 2008. Transfers to this group of immigrants were thus reduced dramatically between 2004 and 2008. This major change was due first and foremost to an improvement in the employment situation, underlining how great an influence employment status has on net transfers.

In Denmark as in other Western countries, immigrants from non-Western countries are often particularly hard hit during periods of recession. In this way, immigrants constitute a group that bears a significant portion of the cost (in the form of increased unemployment and lower earnings) during periods of economic downturn. Periods of economic prosperity and factors that improve the integration of immigrants onto the labour market can therefore greatly reduce net transfers from the public finances to non-Western immigrants.

Table 4. Predicted net transfers per person in DKK, 2005-2008. Amounts in 1997 prices are stated in italics.

	2005	2006	2007	2008
Danes	31,300	34,400	37,700	38,300
	26,500	*28,500*	*30,700*	*30,200*
Immigrants and second-generation immigrants from Western countries	28,100	29,700	30,900	34,400
	23,700	*24,600*	*25,200*	*27,100*
Immigrants and second-generation immigrants from non-Western countries	-53,300	-46,000	-37,800	-31,200
	-45,000	*-38,100*	*-30,800*	*-24,600*

Source: Own calculations based on the Danish Finance Ministry's Law Model and registers at Statistics Denmark.

Refugees do not immigrate to the host country in order to find employment, and they do not necessarily have the type of education and work experience which is in demand on the Danish labour market. It is therefore often more difficult for refugees to find work. Consequently, it is interesting to see what the results are if we exclude the refugees and members of their families from the calculations.[9] These results are shown in Table 5, where refugees are excluded from both the 2004-estimation and the predictions for the years 2005-2008. The groups remaining in the calculations are primarily labour immigrants and family

---

9 For the definition of a refugee used here, see Appendix 1.

reunification immigrants who were not members of the families of refugees. Since refugees as defined here do not form part of the groups of Danes or Western immigrants, the projected net transfers for these groups are unchanged. In contrast, the average amount is markedly less negative for immigrants from non-Western countries when refugees are excluded from that group. For the year 2005, the average net transfers for non-Western immigrants are reduced on this basis from DKK -53,300 to DKK -38,000. Moreover, the amount of transfers falls throughout the period, and reaches a low point of DKK -12,800 in 2008. The improvement in conditions on the labour market had a large effect.

Table 5. Predicted net transfers per person in DKK (excluding refugees), 2005-2008. Amounts in 1997 prices are stated in italics.

	2005	2006	2007	2008
Danes	31,300	34,400	37,700	38,300
	26,500	*28,500*	*30,700*	*30,200*
Immigrants and second-generation immigrants from Western countries	28,100	29,700	30,900	34,400
	23,700	*24,600*	*25,200*	*27,100*
Immigrants and second-generation immigrants from non-Western countries	-38,000	-30,500	-21,300	-12,800
	-32,000	*-25,300*	*-17,400*	*-10,100*

Source: Own calculations based on the Danish Finance Ministry's Law Model and registers at Statistics Denmark.

In the next stage, we examine the total amount of net transfers; the results are presented in Table 6. The calculations were made on the basis of the information in Table 4.

Table 6. Predicted net transfers to public finances (DKK millions), 2005-2008. Amounts in 1997 prices are stated in italics.

	2005	2006	2007	2008
Immigrants and second-generation immigrants from Western countries	2,900 *2,400*	3,200 *2,600*	3,400 *2,700*	3,900 *3,100*
Immigrants and second-generation immigrants from non-Western countries	-12,900 *-10,900*	-11,600 *-9,600*	-10,200 *-8,300*	-9,100 *-7,200*
All immigrants (including second-generation immigrants)	-10,000 *-8,500*	-8,500 *-7,000*	-6,800 *-5,500*	-5,200 *-4,100*
	---Percent of GDP---			
Immigrants and second-generation immigrants from Western countries	0.19	0.19	0.20	0.22
Immigrants and second-generation immigrants from non-Western countries	-0.83	-0.71	-0.60	-0.52
All immigrants (including second-generation immigrants)	-0.64	-0.52	-0.40	-0.30

Source: Own calculations based on the Danish Finance Ministry's Law Model and registers at Statistics Denmark.

As expected, the total calculated net transfers to non-Western immigrants, though still negative, fall sharply over the course of the period 2005-2008. However, the decrease is a little less than in the case of the average net transfers per person, because the number of non-Western immigrants and second-generation immigrants rose during the period. The total net transfers for all immigrants including second-generation immigrants as a proportion of GDP halved over the period 2005-2008, falling from -0.64% to -0.30%.

In the next and final stage of the calculations we show in Table 7 how the total amounts of net transfers change when refugees are excluded from the reckoning. Total net transfers from immigrants to public finances improve over the years and in fact end up being positive, at a figure of DKK 1.7 billion, in 2008.

Table 7. Predicted net transfers to public finances (DKK millions) 2005-2008, with refugees excluded. Amounts in 1997 prices are stated in italics.

	2005	2006	2007	2008
Immigrants and second-generation immigrants from Western countries	2,900 *2,400*	3,200 *2,600*	3,400 *2,700*	3,900 *3,100*
Immigrants and second-generation immigrants from non-Western countries	-5,100 *-4,300*	-4,400 *-3,600*	-3,300 *-2,700*	-2,200 *-1,800*
All immigrants (including second-generation immigrants)	-2,200 *-1,900*	-1,200 *-1,000*	100 *50*	1,700 *1,300*
---------------------- Percent of GDP----------------------				
Immigrants and second-generation immigrants from Western countries	0.19	0.19	0.20	0.22
Immigrants and second-generation immigrants from non-Western countries	-0.33	-0.27	-0.20	-0.13
All immigrants, excluding refugees (including second-generation immigrants)	-0.14	-0.07	0.00	0.10

Source: Own calculations based on the Danish Finance Ministry's Law Model and registers at Statistics Denmark.

There are good grounds to continue this work and analyze which factors contributed most to the change. Factors which may have significance are that a proportion of the immigrants who had not previously been in employment found work thanks to the improved economic conditions; that more of the second-generation immigrants, who constitute a young group, reached an age where many of them began work; and that many of the new labour immigrants who arrived later in the period had work.

10. Summary

International migration can have significant consequences, not just for the migrants themselves, but for the countries they leave and those to which they travel. These consequences may be social, cultural and economic in nature. One of the economic consequences for a recipient country is in terms of the net transfers to public finances from immigrants. The significance of these consequences to the country in a given calendar year is dependent on three factors: 1) the amount of the net transfers for each age level in the year in question, 2) the age composition of the immigrant group and 3) the size of the immigrant group. Migration may also have other, more indirect consequences for public finances; however, these are not considered in the present study.

Redistribution of income via the public finances flows mainly from people of working age to younger and older people. It is therefore reasonable to expect that net transfers from labour immigrants will mostly be positive. Members of this group generally enter the labour market directly. It is a group that is predominantly made up of people of working age, including the family members who come with them. The same is not true for refugee immigrants. These people are admitted to the host country for humanitarian reasons, and on the basis of the same type of arguments that are used to justify overseas aid, and not on the grounds of the prospect of any economic advantage. Refugees may arrive in a country during periods of high unemployment there, and in many cases their education and work experience do not match those needed in the host country.

The results for net transfers to the public finances which we have described supplement data from previous studies in Denmark by supplying figures for the years 2004-2008. As in previous years, net transfers in this period are found to have been made from Western immigrants to the public sector, while the transfers flowed in the opposite direction for non-Western immigrants. Specifically, the net transfers from Western immigrants and second-generation immigrants to the public finances are calculated as being around DKK 2.6 billion in 2004, as compared with DKK -12.8 billion for non-Western immigrants and second-generation immigrants. The corresponding figures for 2008 are DKK 3.9 billion and DKK -9.1 billion for Western and non-Western immigrants respectively. It must be borne in mind, however, that refugees make up a large proportion of the latter group. We have therefore carried out a supplementary calculation in which refugees and their families are not included. This shows that net transfers to the remaining non-Western immigrants and second-generation immigrants amount to only DKK -2.2 billion.

Employment opportunities improved greatly in Denmark over the period 2004-2008, for non-Western immigrants as well as for other people. This also led to a considerable reduction in net transfers to non-Western immigrants, underlining the importance of pursuing economic policies that maintain unemployment rates at a low level.

Appendix 1. Definition of refugees

In this study, refugees are defined on the basis of their country of origin and, in some cases, their year of arrival in Denmark. This definition is very similar to that used in Damm (2003) and Hummelgaard et al. (1995).

In the analyses, a person is defined as a refugee if he or she is an immigrant to Denmark and comes from one of the countries listed below.

Refugee countries

Irrespective of year of migration: Afghanistan, Iraq, Vietnam, stateless
After 1980: Iran
After 1984: Sri Lanka
After 1988: Somalia
After 1991: Former Yugoslavia (Bosnia-Herzegovina, Serbia-Montenegro, Croatia, Macedonia)
Before 1989: Poland
Before 1991: Ethiopia

Second-generation refugees

Second-generation immigrants from the following countries are defined as second-generation refugees:
Afghanistan, Iraq, Vietnam, Stateless, Iran, Sri Lanka, Somalia, Former Yugoslavia (Bosnia-Herzegovina, Serbia-Montenegro, Croatia, Macedonia), Poland, Ethiopia.

Gloss

Stateless: A group consisting primarily of Palestinians from Lebanon.

Damm (2003) states that 90 percent of the refugees who arrived in Denmark during the period 1986-1998 came from the countries listed above. Since refugees are very frequently joined by dependents from the same countries in the process of family reunification, later arrivals from these countries are regarded in the analysis as arriving for family reunification with refugees. Poles are an important exception to this principle. Poles are not counted as refugees (or dependents of refugees arriving for family reunification) if they arrived in Denmark after the fall of the Berlin Wall in 1989.

References

Ablett, John (1999). 'Generational Accounting in Australia', in Alan J. Auerbach, Laurence J. Kotlikoff and Willi Leibfritz (eds), *Generational Accounting Around the World*, Chicago: The University of Chicago Press.

Akbari, Ather H. (1991). 'The Public Finance Impact of Immigrant Population on Host Nations: Some Canadian Evidence', *Social Science Quarterly*, Vol. 2, no. 2, pp. 334-46.

Auerbach, Alan J. and Philip Oreopoulos (1999). 'Generational Accounting and Immigration in the United States'. NBER Working Papers 7041, March.

Bodvarsson, Örn B. and Hendrik Van den Berg (2009), *The Economics of Immigration: Theory and Policy*, Berlin, Heidelberg: Springer Verlag.

Bonin, Holger (2002). 'Eine fiskalische Gesamtbilanz der Zuwanderung nach Deutschland', *Vierteljahreshefte zur Wirtschaftsforschung*, Vol. 71, no. 2, pp. 215-229.

Bonin, Holger, Bernd Raffelhüschen and Jan Walliser (2000). 'Can Immigration Alleviate the Demographic Burden?' *Finanzarchiv*, Vol 57, no. 1, pp. 1-21.

Clune, Michael P. (1998). 'The Fiscal Impacts of Immigrants: A California Case Study', in James P. Smith and Barry Edmonston (eds), *The Immigration Debate. Studies on the Economic, Demographic, and Fiscal Effects of Immigration*. Washington, D.C.: National Academy Press.

Collado, M. Dolores, Iñigo Iturbe-Ormaetye and Guadalupe Valera (2004). 'Quantifying the Impact of Immigration on the Spanish Welfare State'. *International Tax and Public Finance*, Vol. 11, pp. 335-353.

Damm, Anna Piil (2003). *Dispersal Policies, Geographical Settlement and Labour Market Outcomes of Immigrants*. PhD Thesis. Aarhus School of Business.

Danmarks Statistik (2010). *Indvandrere i Danmark 2010*.

ECON (1996). *Innvandring og offentlig økonomi*. Report 46/96, Oslo: ECON.

Ekberg, Jan (1983). *Inkomsteffekter av invandring*. Acta Wexionensia, Serie 2, Economy and Politics, Växjö.

Ekberg, Jan (1999). 'Immigration and the public sector: Income effects for the native population in Sweden', *Journal of Population Economics*, Vol. 12, no. 3, pp. 278-97.

Ekberg, Jan (2009). *Invandringen och de offentliga finanserna*. Rapport till Expertgruppen för studier i offentlig ekonomi, 2009:3.

Garvey, Deborah L. and Thomas J. Espenshade (1998). 'Fiscal Impacts of Immigrant and Native Households: A New Jersey Case Study', in James P. Smithand Barry Edmonston (eds), *The Immigration Debate. Studies on the Economic, Demographic, and Fiscal Effects of Immigration*. Washington, D.C.: National Academy Press.

Gerdes, Christer and Eskil Wadensjö (2006). *Immigration and the Welfare State: Some Danish Experience*. AMID Working Paper 60/2006.

Gustafsson, Björn and Torun Österberg (2001). 'Immigrants and the public sector budget – accounting exercises for Sweden', *Journal of Population Economics*, Vol. 14, no. 4, pp. 689-708.

Hummelgaard, Hans, Leif Husted, Anders Holm, Mikkel Baadsgaard and Benedicte Olrik. 1995. *Etniske minoriteter, integration og mobilitet*. København: AKF-forlag

Larsen, Knut Arild and Erik Bruce (1998). 'Virkninger av innvandring på de offentlige finanser i Norge', in Torben Bager and Shahamak Rezaei (eds), *Invandringens økonomiske konsekvenser i Skandinavien*. Esbjerg: Sydjysk Universitetsforlag.

Lee, Ronald and Timothy Miller (1998). 'The Current Fiscal Impact of Immigrants and their Descendants: Beyond the Immigrant Household', in James P. Smith and Barry Edmonston (eds), *The Immigration Debate. Studies on the Economic, Demographic, and Fiscal Effects of Immigration*. Washington, D.C.: National Academy Press.

Lundby Hansen, Mads (2011). *Negativt nettobidrag på 16 Mia. Kr på de offentlige finanser fra indvandrere og efterkommere fra mindre udviklede lande – potentiale for forbedring*. København: CEPOS.

MaCurdy, Thomas, Thomas Nechyba and Jay Bhattacharya (1998). 'An Economic Framework for Assessing the Fiscal Impacts of Immigration', in James P. Smith and Barry Edmonston (eds), *The Immigration Debate. Studies on the Economic, Demographic, and Fiscal Effects of Immigration.* Washington, D.C.: National Academy Press.

Malchow-Møller, Nikolaj, Jakob Roland Munch og Jan Rose Skaksen (2009). *Det danske arbejdsmarked og EU-udvidelsen mod øst.* Copenhagen: Gyldendal.

Moscarola, Flavia Coda (2001). *The Effects of Immigration Inflow on the Sustainability of the Italian Welfare State*. CeRP Working Paper 6/01.

Pekkala Kerr, Sari and William R. Kerr (2011), *Economic Impacts of Immigration*. NBER Working Paper 16736.

Rothman, Eric S. and Thomas J. Espenshade (1992). 'Fiscal Impacts of Immigration to the United States', *Population Index*, Vol. 58, no. 3, pp. 318-415.

Simon, Julian L. (1984). 'Immigrants, Taxes, and Welfare in the United States', *Population and Development Review*, Vol. 10, no. 1, pp. 55-69.

Schultz-Nielsen, Marie Louise (2010). 'Essays in Migration and Fertility'. *PhD thesis. 2010:1.* Aarhus School of Business.

Storesletten, Kjetil (1998). 'Nettoeffekten av invandringen på offentliga finanser – en nuvärdesberäkning för Sverige', in Torben Bager and Shahamak Rezaei (eds), *Invandringens økonomiske konsekvenser i Skandinavien.* Esbjerg: Sydjysk Universitetsforlag.

Storesletten, Kjetil (2000). 'Sustaining Fiscal Policy through Immigration', *Journal of Political Economy*, Vol. 108, no. 2, pp. 300-23.

Storesletten, Kjetil (2003). 'Fiscal implications of immigration: a net present value calculation', *Scandinavian Journal of Economics,* Vol. 105, no. 3, pp. 487-506.

Tranæs, Torben (ed.) (2008). *Indvandrerne og det danske uddannelsessystem.* Copenhagen: Gyldendal.

Wadensjö, Eskil (1973). *Immigration och samhällsekonomi*. Lund: Studentlitteratur.

Wadensjö, Eskil (2000). 'Immigration, the labour market, and public finances in Denmark', *Swedish Economic Policy Review*, Vol 7, pp. 59-84.

Wadensjö, Eskil (2000a). 'Omfördelning via offentlig sektor: en fördjupad analys', in Gunnar Viby Mogensen and Poul Chr. Matthiessen, *Integration i Danmark omkring årtusindskiftet.* Aarhus: Aarhus University Press.

Wadensjö, Eskil (2007). 'Immigration and the net transfers within the public sector in Denmark', *European Journal of Political Economy*, Vol. 23, no. 2, pp. 472-85.

Wadensjö, Eskil and Helena Orrje (2002). *Immigration and the Public Sector in Denmark.* Aarhus: Aarhus University Press

Wadensjö, Eskil and Christer Gerdes (2004). 'Immigrants and the Public Sector in Denmark and Germany', in Torben Tranæs and Klaus Zimmerman (eds), *Migrants, Work and the Welfare State*. Odense: University Press of Southern Denmark.